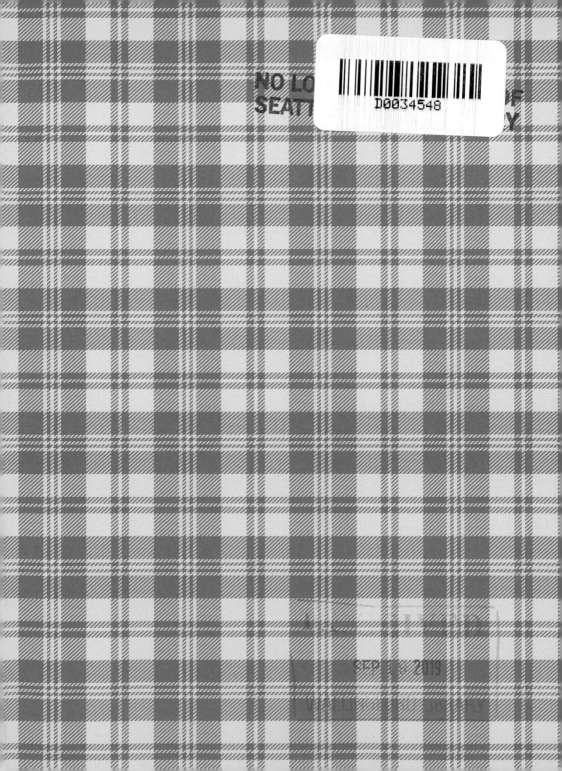

THE

FRIENDSGIVING

HANDBOOK

THE
FRIENDSGIVING
HANDBOOK

Emily Stephenson

Illustrations by
Melanie Gandyra

CHRONICLE BOOKS
SAN FRANCISCO

Library of Congress Cataloging-in-Publication Data:

Names: Stephenson, Emily, author. | Gandyra, Melanie, illustrator.
Title: The friendsgiving handbook / Emily Stephenson ; illustrations by
Melanie Gandyra. Description: San Francisco : Chronicle Books, [2019]
Identifiers: LCCN 2018050504 | ISBN 9781452176949 (hardcover ; alk.
paper) Subjects: LCSH: Thanksgiving cooking. | Entertaining. | Holiday
cooking. Classification: LCC TX739.2.T45 S74 2019 | DDC 641.5/68--
dc23 LC record available at https://lccn.loc.gov/2018050504

Manufactured in China.

Design by Lizzie Vaughan.
Typeset in Brown, Capita, and Buena Park.

10 9 8 7 6 5 4 3 2 1

Chronicle books and gifts are available at special quantity
discounts to corporations, professional associations, literacy
programs, and other organizations. For details and discount
information, please contact our corporate/premiums department
at corporatesales@chroniclebooks.com or at 1-800-759-0190.

Chronicle Books LLC
680 Second Street
San Francisco, California 94107
www.chroniclebooks.com

TO EVERYONE
inspired to feed friends
and share the holiday.

CONTENTS

INTRODUCTION

THANKSGIVING is a remarkable holiday. Devoid of consumerism and religion (mostly), it's a time to get together with people you love and share an extravagant meal. Traditionally that means your family, but increasingly it can mean sharing a meal with your *chosen* family on Thanksgiving or hosting a meal just for friends in advance of the holiday.

I find the statistic that the day before Thanksgiving is the busiest travel day of the year in the United States incredibly heartwarming: all those people traveling for just one meal. But this is also one of the main reasons Friendsgiving exists. As we move farther for work, to more expensive cities, and to jobs with fewer benefits and wages that haven't kept up with inflation, it becomes harder to buy a plane ticket during the most expensive travel period of the year. And—in an unforeseen planning error from governments and churches of yesteryear—it's just one month before the *other* most expensive travel period of the year.

I've been hosting Friendsgiving since 2006 for very practical reasons. I've lived anywhere between one thousand and four thousand miles away from my hometown, and my mom really loves Christmas, so the decision was easy. My first two years away, I tried other Thanksgiving strategies: my freshman year of college I went to what turned out to be a pretty sad restaurant Thanksgiving, and my even sadder sophomore year, I did nothing. After that, I threw my own dinners.

Hosting Friendsgiving is a joy. Most of us never have this kind of elaborate, multicourse meal at any other time of year. It's a chance to show off your hosting skills or try fancier recipes you never have reason to make. Or to spend the better part of the day just being together, since your Friendsgiving might include a morning turkey trot, football game, volunteering shift, or just arriving early to hang out and help. And as much as I do love my extended family, sharing what I'm thankful for with the people who get me through my daily life when I'm far away from relatives feels so special.

After hosting more than ten years of Friendsgivings, I have some things to share. You'll find recipes to get you from the moment the first guest arrives and you're running behind schedule to when everyone couldn't possibly eat another bite but somehow manages to have two slices of pie. You'll find advice on how to plan a menu so not everything needs to be baked at the same time at five different temperatures; how you can do the least as a host (my preference) or how you can do the most; and, of course, how to get everything on the table (relatively) on time. I tried to represent regional Thanksgiving dishes and include something

for every taste. There are plenty of vegetarian recipes, some vegan ones, and three different turkey options, depending on your cooking skills and the time you want to spend. I hope these recipes can become part of your ever-evolving Friendsgiving traditions.

We can't be sure what life will throw our way, and after many years of hosting, I'm starting to see some changes: friends get married and have two families to spend holidays with, others start their own families or leave our expensive city. I know the way my Friendsgivings look will change over the years, and perhaps someday soon they will be a combination of family and friends. But no matter how it ends up happening, it's a wonderful time to build our chosen families and share the most special meal of the year.

Congrats!

You've decided you want to have your friends over for Thanksgiving.

That's very generous of you, and it's going to be a lot of fun. It's also going to be a lot of work (sorry). There are some decisions you need to make as quickly as possible, namely around how the food will get from raw ingredients to your table, fully cooked.

THERE ARE A FEW ROUTES YOU CAN GO:

1 × You Do Everything

A great option for the bighearted and/or control freaks. If you decide to go this route, you'll need to figure out what you'll be cooking and for how many people. For the former, see Plan Like a Pro (page 58).

Unlike other hosting situations, Thanksgiving has a lot of leeway with menu planning. You could make a turkey and all the sides and have enough food for anywhere from six to twenty-five people. If you like to play things fast and loose, you could just send out a group email, cook a ton, and wait to see who shows up. You probably won't run out of food. For the more anxious, invites with an RSVP deadline are the way to go.

2 ✕ You Cook Some Dishes

I think of this as "hosting on a budget." You do a lot, but you don't do everything. I'd recommend providing the turkey and the things that are made with/from the turkey: stuffing and gravy. If you're vegetarian, make the main dish. After that, if it won't feel like Thanksgiving without your aunt's sweet potato casserole or your famous cranberry sauce, then make those, too. Tell guests they can bring something they want to eat, or give them the option to just bring wine.

This is the most chill option because you're basically cooking a mini Thanksgiving dinner and everything else that's brought is gilding the lily. So if everyone brings salad (see Potluck Style) or everyone brings only wine, you'll still have a great meal.

3 ✕ Potluck Style

Learn from my mistakes: One year, I was hosting a group with a pretty high vegetarian count, so I made all the desserts and told everyone else to bring sides. "Easy breezy," I thought to myself. "It's worked out every year before!" We ate twelve salads followed by five kinds of pie. It was a fun Thanksgiving, if not particularly filling.

I promise it's not too much to make a spreadsheet so people can sign up for types of dishes. You'll be happy your one friend signed up for mashed potatoes and your neighbor signed up for green bean casserole instead of eating ten sweet potato dishes. Sorry to sound like your mom, but a little planning goes a long way!

TO START

The
Very Important Question of

What
TO
Drink

||||||||||||||||||||||||||||||||||||||||||||||||||||||||||||||||||||||||||||||||||||||||||||

THANKSGIVING IS AN EPIC MEAL,

during which a crowd can consume
a surprising amount of beverages.

Since the food part of the meal does take a lot of work, make the drink part easy.

Throughout the meal, be sure to have at least one nonalcoholic option besides water, such as cider or punch. I also like to buy a lot of liter bottles of seltzer to have on the table throughout dinner. (Saves on washing—or owning—pitchers.) And mixed with a few dashes of bitters and some leftover Rosemary Simple Syrup (page 21), it makes a refreshing drink.

1× Cocktail Hour

This is kind of an old-school, cheesy way of putting it, and we can keep that title just between us. But having something to get people started while you finish cooking and you're waiting for everyone to arrive makes the evening feel special. Plus, you can just hand the pitcher of your premade drink (page 21) to the first guest, and they can serve everyone else. Depending on how punctual your friends are, or how early you told people to arrive, expect up to two drinks per person.

2× Dinner

I always go for wine during dinner, though you may have some beer drinkers attending who'd prefer otherwise. The easiest and cheapest option is to simply ask everyone to bring something to drink and be done with it. They can do the research and figure out the best wine to pair with Thanksgiving flavors, or buy whatever the food magazines recommend this year. The amounts work out generously—one person, one bottle of wine or six-pack—as long as you're not inviting all couples and the couples only bring one bottle each. (That is, in my experience, not enough wine!) If you're the type of person who wants to provide everything for your guests, buy a case of a wine you like, and don't stress too much about proper pairing. Do the same for beer. Honestly, people just want there to be something drinkable and lots of it.

3× Dessert

If there's ever a time to drink a digestif, it's Thanksgiving. Imagine: a whole category of booze designed to help with that uncomfortable feeling from eating too much! One bottle will go a long way, as it's potent stuff that's not for everyone. But eating a slice of pie with a little pour of amaro, grappa, or brandy is a lovely way to end the night. A box of Underberg (the nonalcoholic option) means everyone can have a drink. Whether they like the flavor is another matter.

THERE ARE two reasons to have a signature cocktail option ready to go at the start of your evening. One, it makes the dinner feel a little more special, even if you're not an at-home-bar kind of person (I'm not). Two, you ensure the first person who shows up has something to drink—in case you outsourced the wine to your guests—and can keep busy pouring cocktails as people arrive.

AND SINCE the last thing you need to be doing is mixing individual cocktails, make a batch in the morning on Thanksgiving (or earlier—it gets better as it sits) and forget about it until the first time your doorbell rings.

Rosemary Old-Fashioneds for a Crowd

ROSEMARY SIMPLE SYRUP

½ cup [100 g] sugar

2 sprigs fresh rosemary

One 750-ml bottle bourbon

20 dashes Angostura bitters

1 orange

5 sprigs fresh rosemary

SERVES
12

MAKE SYRUP AHEAD
3 months

MAKE COCKTAILS AHEAD
1 day

PREP TIME
1½ hours

TO MAKE THE SIMPLE SYRUP: In a small saucepan, mix the sugar with ½ cup [120 ml] water and add the rosemary. Put the pan over medium-high heat and cook, stirring often, so the sugar dissolves into the water. As soon as the mixture comes to a boil, remove from the heat and let steep for 20 minutes. Discard the rosemary and cool to room temperature. Transfer the mixture to an airtight container or use right away. The syrup will keep in the refrigerator for 3 months. Makes ¾ cup [180 ml].

Pour the bottle of bourbon into a large pitcher, add the bitters, 4 oz [120 ml] water, and 5 oz [150 ml] rosemary simple syrup, and stir to combine. Taste and add more simple syrup if you like. Refrigerate the cocktail until ready to serve.

To serve, cut the orange crosswise into thin slices and quarter the slices. Cut the 5 rosemary sprigs into 1 in [2.5 cm] or so pieces. Add a few ice cubes to each glass, pour in 2 oz [60 ml] of the premade cocktail, and garnish with a rosemary sprig and two orange slices. Serve right away.

Fig and Olive Relish

1½ cups [380 g] halved dried figs

2 cups [480 ml] boiling water

1½ cups [180 g] walnuts

1 cup [160 g] pitted oil-cured olives

1 cup [12 g] loosely packed fresh parsley leaves

2 anchovy fillets

1 garlic clove

3 Tbsp freshly squeezed lemon juice

½ tsp freshly ground black pepper

½ cup [120 ml] extra-virgin olive oil

Salt (optional)

Crackers, for serving

≻≻≻

SERVES
16

MAKE AHEAD
3 days

PREP TIME
25 minutes

GF

In a medium heatproof bowl, cover the figs with the boiling water. Let the figs sit until they are soft but not mushy, 8 to 10 minutes. Drain the figs and discard the soaking liquid.

In a small skillet, toast the walnuts over medium-low heat until they are golden and smell delicious, 8 to 10 minutes.

Put the walnuts, olives, parsley, anchovies, garlic, lemon juice, and pepper in a food processor (or mortar and pestle) and pulse until everything is finely chopped (you can also do this by hand). Turn on the machine and pour in the olive oil until you have a thick, chunky paste—you don't want it to be smooth. Add the figs and pulse a few times so they're chopped but not puréed.

Taste the mixture and add salt if necessary (between the olives and anchovies it shouldn't be). Transfer to a dish and serve with crackers, or store In an airtight container and refrigerate for up to 3 days. Let the spread come to room temperature before serving.

THERE ARE a lot of carbs and saturated fats coming down the pipeline, so I like to keep the appetizers light and flavorful. This relish is sweet, salty, and intense (in a good way) from the anchovies and garlic. It's great with apples, crackers, and even cheese, if you're in the mood for more dairy. I serve it because it's so different from anything to come on the menu, but leftovers are also pretty good spread on toasted bread for a turkey sandwich.

BESIDES TRYING to avoid bread and butter (see: the rest of the meal), appetizers should be *easy*. And nothing's easier than these fried and lightly scented almonds. They take 15 minutes to make, which is a lot less time than all of the dishes that will come after it. Also, I'd happily eat an entire bowl of fried sage leaves if I could.

Sage Fried Almonds

½ cup [120 ml]
extra-virgin olive oil

½ cup [6 g] loosely packed
fresh sage leaves

4 cups [560 g] raw almonds

2 tsp paprika (not smoked)

2 tsp salt

> >

SERVES
14

MAKE AHEAD
1 day

PREP TIME
15 minutes

Line a medium bowl with paper towels. In a large skillet, heat the oil over medium heat until it shimmers, but don't let it smoke. Add the sage leaves in two or three batches (so they don't burn as you fish them out) and fry until they are dark green and fragrant, about 1 minute. Use a slotted spoon to transfer the sage leaves to the prepared bowl.

Add the almonds to the pan and cook, stirring often, until they are golden, shiny, and smell delicious but don't take on much color (otherwise they'll keep cooking off the heat and burn), 3 to 5 minutes. Add the paprika, stir, then immediately use a slotted spoon to transfer the almonds to the prepared bowl to drain. Quickly remove the paper towels, add the salt, and toss to evenly distribute the seasoning.

Let cool to room temperature, then serve or store in an airtight container for up to 24 hours.

TO START

THESE BUTTERY rolls are great for accompanying your Thanksgiving meal, or getting a little ahead of yourself and making mini turkey sandwiches on the day of.

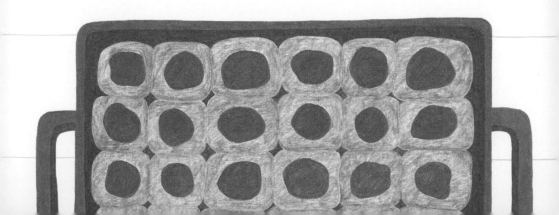

Pull-Apart Rolls

2 tsp active dry yeast

¾ cup [180 ml] whole milk

7 Tbsp [100 g] unsalted butter

3 Tbsp sugar

1 tsp kosher salt

3 cups [420 g] all-purpose flour, plus more as needed

Flaky sea salt

SERVES

16

PREP TIME

2½ hours

In a small bowl, whisk the yeast and 3 Tbsp water that's a little warmer than body temperature (about 115°F [45°C]). Let the mixture sit until it's bubbly and the yeast has dissolved.

In a small saucepan, heat the milk, 5 Tbsp [70 g] of the butter, the sugar, and kosher salt until the sugar has dissolved. If the mixture gets too hot, let it cool down to the same temperature as the water for the yeast. Pour the mixture into a large bowl and add the yeast mixture. Whisk with a fork to combine.

Add the flour and stir until the dough forms a slightly sticky ball. If the mixture is very wet, add more flour about 1 Tbsp at a time and knead. Repeat until the dough just barely sticks to your hands. If the mixture is too dry, sprinkle with a few drops of water and knead until the dough is just tacky.

Lightly flour your work surface and dump the dough out. Flour your hands and knead the dough until it is smooth and springy (if you press the dough, the indent will bounce back). Cover the dough with a towel and let it rise until it has doubled in size, 30 minutes to 1 hour, depending on how hot your kitchen is. (Alternatively, if you need your work surface for something else, you can put the dough in a lightly oiled bowl and cover with a towel.)

cont'd

Preheat the oven to 350°F [180°C]. Grease a 9 in [23 cm] square pan with butter. Divide the dough into sixteen pieces: you can either eyeball it or weigh out roughly 1½ oz [45 g] balls. Evenly space the dough balls in the buttered dish. Cover the pan with a towel and let the dough rise again for 30 minutes. In a small saucepan, melt the remaining 2 Tbsp butter. Brush the risen dough with half of the melted butter.

Bake the rolls until they have puffed up and are golden brown, 25 to 30 minutes. Brush the tops with the remaining butter, sprinkle with the flaky salt, and serve warm.

Butter

(and Other Ingredients)

THERE IS A LOT OF BUTTER IN THIS BOOK.
CONSIDER YOURSELF WARNED.

I don't cook with butter throughout the rest of the year, but Thanksgiving doesn't feel like itself without rich food. Butter is used in nearly every recipe. Since it's a once-a-year holiday, I'm OK with that. I usually eat leftovers for two days max, and then it's back to my less dairy-heavy life.

However, if you are alarmed at how rich the food here is, or if you're cooking for any vegans, there are plenty of recipes—such as the vegetable sides—where it can be swapped out for olive oil. In fact, for everything but the pie crust, you can substitute oil and it will still taste delicious.

Speaking of vegans (and vegetarians), you'll notice that a lot of recipes list chicken stock or dry white wine. I consider the latter the vegetarian option. I have yet to find a boxed vegetable stock that tastes good. Or, honestly, homemade stock. It's fine, but I don't want my whole dish to taste like it. You can also substitute water for stock or wine in any of the recipes, just add a little more of the other seasonings to make up for it.

Finally, all salt is kosher salt, specifically Diamond Crystal. Please note that Morton brand kosher salt is much saltier, as is sea salt. You can find plenty of conversion guides online, though I heartily recommend Diamond Crystal for your all-purpose salt.

ON THE SIDE

Tablescaping

———

I'm no Sandra Lee, but doing

A LITTLE
SOMETHING
EXTRA

for Thanksgiving is mandatory.

At the Very Least

✕ Make sure you have enough plates, cutlery, glasses, and serving vessels (they don't have to be nice serving vessels, but you need *something* for each dish).

✕ Put a tablecloth down. The darker the better, really. As nice as white looks, it's not going to survive the night.

✕ Light a few candles. Tea lights are fine.

Extra Credit

✕ Add a little something to decorate the table: embrace decorative gourd season, get those branches the design magazines always show, or put out a bouquet or two of flowers.

✕ Upgrade your place settings: cloth napkins, matching plates, real wineglasses.

✕ Invest in dedicated tableware. I have nothing against serving gravy in a glass measuring cup and side dishes in their pots, but if you want to get a gravy boat or serving bowls, now's the time.

Friendsgiving Superstar Status

✕ Be the extra host you're dying to be: Make a seating chart. With place cards. (I've never done this; let me know how it goes.)

Chicory and Apple Salad with Sherry Vinaigrette

SHERRY VINAIGRETTE

¼ cup [60 ml] sherry vinegar

2 Tbsp minced shallot

1 tsp salt, plus more for seasoning

1 tsp sugar, or 1 Tbsp honey

½ cup [120 ml] extra-virgin olive oil

2 tsp Dijon mustard

¼ tsp freshly ground black pepper

SALAD

1 head radicchio, trimmed and chopped

1 head Belgian endive, trimmed and chopped

1 head escarole or frisée, trimmed and chopped

2 sweet, crisp apples, halved, cored, and thinly sliced

Salt and freshly ground black pepper

>>

SERVES
8 to 12

MAKE DRESSING AHEAD
1 week

PREP TIME
30 minutes

TO MAKE THE VINAIGRETTE: Put the vinegar, shallot, salt, and sugar in an 8 oz [240 ml] jar. Let the shallots pickle for at least an hour at room temperature and up to 2 days in the refrigerator. Add the olive oil, mustard, and pepper to the jar. Seal tightly, then shake vigorously until the vinaigrette is emulsified. Taste and add more salt and pepper if necessary. The vinaigrette will keep in the refrigerator for up to 1 week.

TO MAKE THE SALAD: In a large bowl—the largest you have!—combine the greens and apples, and season with salt and pepper. Shake the dressing again and drizzle about half over the salad. Toss the salad and taste, adding more dressing if you like. Serve within the hour, since it will sit as the meal goes on.

SALAD IS not the first dish that you might associate with Thanksgiving, but it's nice to have a break from the soft, rich foods that make up the rest of the meal. The bitter greens, sweet apples, and sharp vinaigrette provide a welcome break for your palate and give some texture to your plate. The added bonus with chicories is that they can stand up to dressing for hours without wilting, just in case the salad sits a little more neglected than other offerings, or you end up with leftovers for the day after (it'd be great on a turkey sandwich).

TRY TO find a crisp and sweet apple variety, such as Honeycrisp, Jonagold, Gala, or similar, that's available in your area, and avoid anything overly tart, like Granny Smith.

I KICK off Thanksgiving week every year by making cranberry sauce. I'll come home from my epic grocery shopping trip, put away all the food, and unwind while making cranberry sauce. I do it first thing because it's insanely easy, it can sit in the fridge forever and gets better with time, and it gets me excited for the holiday. It's only one thing to cross off on your (long) to-do list, but sometimes the first task is the most important.

Cranberry Sauce with Candied Ginger

1½ lb [680 g] fresh cranberries

1½ cups [360 ml] dry red wine (or orange juice)

1½ cups [300 g] lightly packed light brown sugar

½ cup [70 g] minced candied ginger

>>

SERVES
10 to 12

MAKE AHEAD
1 week

PREP TIME
1 hour

In a large saucepan, combine all the ingredients and stir. Cook over medium heat, stirring occasionally, until all the cranberries have popped, 20 to 30 minutes. If you prefer a more jam-like sauce, continue cooking for up to 15 minutes longer. Let the mixture cool to room temperature, and then transfer to an airtight container and store in the refrigerator for up to 1 week. Serve at room temperature.

Guest Management

THE MOST IMPORTANT PART OF
FRIENDSGIVING IS YOUR FRIENDS

(it says it right there in the name).

But that doesn't
mean they
can't make things
a little more
difficult for you.

Here are a few
rules to help things
run smoothly...

THINGS TO TELL THEM BEFORE THE DAY:

✕ Don't bring soup. You don't want to wash dinner plates, dessert plates, and bowls for everyone.

✕ They can't cook in your kitchen. Dishes can be warmed up in the oven, but no one else is allowed to chop, sauté, or roast in your kitchen. You've got enough going on.

✕ BYO Tupperware, if leftover distribution is happening.

THINGS FOR YOU TO KEEP IN MIND:

✕ Find out if anyone coming has a food allergy, and let other people cooking know, if needed.

✕ They'll inevitably want to hang out in the kitchen, which is fun if you're feeling good and have everything under control; if not…

✕ Give them something to do while you finish cooking. I've found that having paper and markers on the table to make hand turkeys is an activity that even the most aloof adult in the room eventually participates in. Cocktails help, too.

✕ Do let them help clean up. I'm usually an I-wash-the-dishes-when-everyone-leaves-because-otherwise-it's-a-buzzkill kind of person, but not on Thanksgiving. There are just too many dishes. In fact, this would be a great time to sit back and let everyone else do all of them. You deserve it.

PEOPLE CAN feel very strongly about what defines cornbread! As a midwesterner, I like mine with a hint of sweetness and pretty fluffy. I want to be able to eat it on its own, basically like savory cake. This is a tangy, peppery version that will make a nice addition to any spread.

Black Pepper Cornbread

¾ cup [165 g] unsalted butter, cut into pieces

¼ cup [85 g] honey

2 cups [480 ml] buttermilk

3 eggs

1 tsp black peppercorns

1½ cups [200 g fine, or 220 g medium] cornmeal

1 cup [140 g] all-purpose flour

1 Tbsp baking powder

2 tsp salt

½ tsp baking soda

>>

SERVES

12

MAKE AHEAD

4 hours

PREP TIME

1 hour

VEG

Preheat the oven to 375°F [190°C].

Put the butter in a 10 or 11 in [25 or 28 cm] cast-iron or other ovenproof skillet, and put the skillet in the oven. Keep an eye on the butter, and when it has melted, carefully remove the pan from the oven. Pour the melted butter into a large bowl, leaving a generous amount in the skillet. Use a paper towel to carefully butter the pan. Add the honey and buttermilk to the bowl with the butter and whisk to combine. If the mixture is still hot, let it cool to room temperature, then whisk in the eggs.

In a mortar and pestle, spice grinder, or zip-top bag with a rolling pin, crack the peppercorns so that all are at least partially broken, but varied in size. Put the pepper in a medium bowl with the cornmeal, flour, baking powder, salt, and baking soda, and stir with a fork.

cont'd

Add the dry ingredients to the wet ingredients and gently stir until just combined (it's OK if there are a few lumps). Carefully spread the batter in the hot skillet and put the pan back into the oven.

Bake until a toothpick or knife inserted into the center comes out clean and the top is golden brown, 30 to 45 minutes. Remove the skillet from the oven and put on a cooling rack. Slice the cornbread and serve warm or at room temperature.

Stuffing Variation

Instead of a skillet, heat the butter in a rimmed baking sheet. Spread the batter evenly in the sheet and bake until golden around the edges, 18 to 20 minutes. Cut into 1 in [2.5 cm] cubes to use for the dressing recipe on page 70.

Creamed Kale and Collards

2 Tbsp plus 2 tsp salt

1½ lb [680 g] collard greens

1½ lb [680 g] kale
(any variety except purple)

3 Tbsp unsalted butter

2 shallots, chopped

4 garlic cloves, thinly sliced

½ tsp freshly ground black pepper

1 cup [240 ml] chicken stock or dry white wine

3 Tbsp all-purpose flour

¾ cup [180 ml] heavy cream

¾ cup [180 ml] whole milk

1 cup [100 g] grated Parmesan cheese

Large pinch of freshly grated nutmeg

SERVES

8 to 12

MAKE AHEAD

3 days

PREP TIME

1 hour

VEG

Fill a stockpot with at least 3 qt [2.8 L] water and bring to a boil, then add 2 Tbsp of the salt. Separate the leaves and stems of the collards and kale. Chop the stems into small pieces, and roughly chop or tear the leaves.

When the water boils, add some of the chopped leaves (you'll need to work in batches), and cook until they have wilted and are bright green, just a few minutes. Use a slotted spoon or tongs to fish out the greens and transfer to a colander. Repeat with all the greens. Rinse with cold water just until they are cool enough to handle, then squeeze out as much water as you can. Chop the squeezed greens into bite-size pieces and reserve.

In a large Dutch oven, melt the butter over medium heat, then add the shallots, garlic, and chopped stems, and season with the remaining 2 tsp salt and the pepper. Cook, stirring occasionally, until the shallots are translucent, 6 to 8 minutes. Add the stock and cook until it has completely evaporated, 7 to 10 minutes. Add the flour and cook, stirring often, until the flour and butter are fully incorporated and the mixture is a light golden color, 3 to 5 minutes.

cont'd

EVEN HEALTHY greens need to be decadent on Thanksgiving. This is a heartier, more autumnal upgrade to creamed spinach that's always part of my spread.

Pour in the cream and milk, and adjust the heat to medium-low. Cook, stirring often and scraping the bottom of the pan to loosen any flour, until the sauce is steaming and has thickened enough to coat the back of a spoon, 2 to 5 minutes. Don't let it boil, and lower the heat if it's starting to bubble and is not yet thickened. Add the Parmesan and nutmeg, and stir to fully incorporate. Fold in the greens. Taste and adjust the seasoning. At this point you can cool the mixture and refrigerate for up to 3 days. Reheat gently in a pot over medium-low heat before serving, taking care not to let the bottom scorch.

I MADE a variation of this dish for a family Thanksgiving (so long ago I hadn't even started hosting Friendsgiving) and my aunt *still* talks about it. It changed her from a Brussels sprouts hater to a lover. Make this a part of your dinner so you can convert any lingering holdouts.

Sautéed Brussels Sprouts with Pine Nuts

2½ lb [1.2 kg] Brussels sprouts

1 lemon, halved

½ cup [60 g] pine nuts

3 Tbsp extra-virgin olive oil

1 Tbsp unsalted butter

3 garlic cloves, minced or grated

1 tsp red pepper flakes

⅓ cup [80 ml] dry white wine

2 tsp salt, plus more for seasoning

½ tsp freshly ground black pepper, plus more for seasoning

½ cup [20 g] chopped fresh parsley

>>>

SERVES

12

PREP BRUSSELS SPROUTS AHEAD

6 hours

PREP TIME

30 minutes

Trim the bottom stems from the Brussels sprouts and reserve any whole leaves that separate in the process. If you have a food processor, use the slicing attachment to slice the sprouts and transfer them to a large bowl. If not, use a mandoline or knife to thinly slice the Brussels sprouts (lengthwise or horizontally are both fine). If you're not cooking them right away, toss them with the juice of half a lemon and refrigerate, covered, for up to 6 hours.

In a large skillet over medium-low heat, toast the pine nuts until they are golden and smell delicious but are not burned, 7 to 10 minutes. Immediately transfer to a small bowl.

Raise the heat to high and return the skillet to the burner. Heat the olive oil, butter, garlic, and red pepper flakes just until fragrant, about 30 seconds. Add the Brussels sprouts, wine, salt, and pepper. Cook, stirring constantly as best you can (there's a lot of food!), until the sprouts are just a little wilted and the wine has mostly cooked off, 5 to 7 minutes.

Remove the pan from the heat and add the juice from the remaining lemon half. Taste and adjust the seasoning. Stir in the pine nuts and parsley, and serve right away, or keep the nuts and parsley separate and keep warm for up to 30 minutes. Stir in the nuts and parsley before serving.

Roasted Pumpkin with Bacon and Dates

One 4 to 6 lb [1.8 to 2.7 kg] sugar pumpkin, or other small pumpkin variety

Small bunch fresh thyme sprigs

3 Tbsp extra-virgin olive oil

2 tsp salt

1 tsp freshly ground black pepper

6 bacon slices, chopped

8 dates, pitted and sliced

¼ cup [60 ml] sherry or red wine vinegar

SERVES

12

PREP TIME

1 hour

GF

Preheat the oven to 425°F [220°C].

Halve the pumpkin vertically by cutting on one side of the stem. It won't be perfectly in half, but that's fine. Use a spoon to scrape the seeds and fibers out of the cavity and discard. Cut the halves into wedges no larger than 1 in [2.5 cm] at the widest part.

Put the pumpkin wedges in a large bowl and add the thyme, oil, salt, and pepper; toss to coat. Spread the pumpkin slices on a rimmed baking sheet in a single layer so each wedge can get nice and browned.

Bake the pumpkin, undisturbed, until it's tender and browned on the bottom, 35 to 45 minutes. Transfer the pumpkin to a serving platter.

In a large, nonreactive skillet, cook the bacon and dates over medium-high heat, stirring often, until the bacon is crisp, 10 to 15 minutes. Pour off as much or as little of the fat as you like, then add the vinegar and scrape any browned bits off the bottom of the pan. Pour the mixture over the pumpkin and serve warm or at room temperature.

IS THE bacon and date combo a little basic and very 2004? Yes. But since everything comes back around, consider this ahead of the trend. Even your most in-the-know friends probably won't care once they take a bite.

Panfried Green Beans with Mushrooms

---

12 oz [340 g] cremini mushrooms, quartered

1 large shallot, halved and sliced

1½ lb [680 g] fresh green beans, trimmed

¾ cup [180 ml] chicken stock or dry white wine

4 Tbsp [55 g] unsalted butter

2 tsp salt, plus more for seasoning

½ tsp freshly ground black pepper

>>

SERVES

8

PREP TIME

30 minutes

In a large, wide skillet over high heat, put the mushrooms and shallots on the bottom, then add the green beans, stock, butter, and salt, and bring the stock to a boil. Cook the vegetables, turning occasionally with tongs, until the beans are bright green and crisp-tender and the stock has mostly evaporated, 12 to 15 minutes. If the green beans are still mostly raw when the liquid has cooked off, add more stock or water 2 Tbsp at a time and continue to cook until they're ready.

Turn the heat down to medium-high and cook, shaking the pan occasionally, until the mushrooms are golden brown on one side, 2 to 5 minutes. At this point the pan should be dry.

Turn off the heat, add the pepper, taste, and add more salt if necessary. Serve right away or cover the pan and keep warm for up to 30 minutes.

THIS HAS all the best parts of green bean casserole without weighing you down (the rest of the meal will do that). The steam-fry method means everything comes together in a snap while the beans stay… snappy (sorry). This dish should be made last minute, but it frees up oven space, and I promise, you really can't mess it up.

Plan LIKE A Pro

||||||||||||||||||||||||||||||||||||||||||||||||||||||||||||||||||||||||||||||||||||||||||||||||||||

I'm guessing that if you're the kind of person who wants to invite a crowd over for the most important meal of the year, then you probably love planning.

IF NOT, you're going to have to do a little so the day goes smoothly. See How to Have All This Food Ready at the Same Time (page 96) for specific cooking tips.

MENU PLANNING

You're the boss and whatever you want goes!

The only things I would suggest keeping in mind are having a mix of stovetop and oven recipes to prevent a cooking traffic jam, and watching your seasonings. That means don't choose recipes that use eight different herbs and four kinds of cheese when you could choose ones that all use thyme, sage, and Parmesan. Then make sure at least half of those dishes can be made on the stovetop or require no cooking; baking is time intensive, and you can only cook one thing at a time.

SHOPPING

Once you have your recipes picked out, make your shopping list.

I get very detail oriented and make a shopping list with the exact amounts of things I need so I can round up at the store (i.e., 3 sticks plus 6 Tbsp butter). Shop the weekend before Thanksgiving. Any earlier and some food might go bad; any later and you run the risk of getting behind schedule. Yes, every store will be packed; you'll just need your game face on.

DINNER ITINERARY

This just means having a dinnertime and an arrival time for guests and making sure it's clearly communicated which is which.

You don't want to tell people dinner starts at 5 p.m. when that means "table is set and food is ready at 5 p.m." Someone is going to be late and you're going to be annoyed. Assume your friends need at least an hour to arrive and get settled, but they also might get antsy after two hours of cocktails and snacks.

THIS IS a simple side dish, though here "simple" means very rich and delicious. And if it's *really* not Thanksgiving for you without toasted marshmallows and sweet potatoes, see Sweet Potato Pie with Marshmallow Fluff on page 113.

Sweet Potatoes au Gratin

1½ cups [360 ml] heavy cream

3 springs fresh sage

3 garlic cloves

3 lb [1.4 kg] sweet potatoes, peeled

1 tsp salt

½ tsp freshly ground pepper

1 cup [100 g] grated Parmesan cheese

>>>

SERVES
12

ASSEMBLE AHEAD
2 days

PREP TIME
1½ hours

VEG

GF

Preheat the oven to 400°F [200°C]. Butter a 9 by 13 in [23 by 33 cm] baking dish.

In a small saucepan, combine the cream, sage, and garlic, and heat over medium-low heat until just steaming. Do not let it boil. Turn off the heat and let the cream steep while you slice the potatoes.

Use a mandoline or the sharpest knife you have to cut the potatoes crosswise into ⅛ in [3 mm] slices. Arrange the slices in the prepared pan by shingling them like fallen dominoes. Pour the cream mixture into the pan, and then sprinkle the potatoes with the salt and pepper. Cover the pan with aluminum foil. At this point, the pan can be refrigerated for up to 2 days. Let it sit out for 30 minutes to take the chill off before proceeding.

Bake the gratin for 35 minutes, undisturbed. Then, carefully remove the foil and the sage and garlic, and add the cheese in an even layer. Continue baking until the mixture is bubbling and the potatoes are very tender when poked with a knife, 15 to 20 minutes longer. Let the gratin set for at least 10 minutes before slicing and serving.

Crème Fraîche and Leek Mashed Potatoes

3 Tbsp unsalted butter

1 lb [455 g] leeks, cleaned, white and light green parts chopped

1 cup [240 ml] chicken stock or water

3 Tbsp plus 1 tsp salt, plus more for seasoning

3 lb [1.4 kg] Yukon Gold potatoes, peeled

1 cup [240 g] crème fraîche

½ to ¾ cup [120 to 180 ml] whole milk

½ tsp freshly ground black pepper, plus more for seasoning

>>>

SERVES
8 to 12

PREP LEEKS AHEAD
3 days

PREP TIME
1 hour

VEG

GF

In a large skillet, melt 1 Tbsp of the butter over medium-high heat. Add the leeks, stock, and 1 tsp of the salt, and bring the mixture to a boil. Adjust the heat so the mixture simmers and cook, stirring occasionally, until the stock has cooked off and the leeks are very tender, 30 to 35 minutes. Remove from the heat. (At this point you can cool the mixture and refrigerate for up to 3 days. Gently heat over medium-low heat before proceeding.)

Meanwhile, in the largest pot you have, bring plenty of water to a boil and add the remaining 3 Tbsp salt. Cut the potatoes into 1 in [2.5 cm] chunks, and add them to the water. Cook until they are very tender but not yet falling apart (you should be able to pierce a piece with a knife and have it easily come back out), 15 to 20 minutes. Drain the potatoes.

Put the remaining 2 Tbsp butter in a small saucepan and melt over low heat. Remove from the heat, and stir in the crème fraîche and ½ cup [120 ml] milk, or up to ¾ cup [180 ml], depending on how loose you like your potatoes.

cont'd

THIS IS a tangy, rich mashed potato recipe that's still neutral enough to go with everything else on your plate. The leeks give it a fall flavor and make the potatoes good enough to eat alone.

AS SIMPLE as mashed potatoes might seem, they're actually kind of tricky to do right. Make sure you use a ricer—or the hack mentioned—so they don't get gummy, and use only Yukon Gold potatoes. Thankfully, pretty much any place that sells potatoes will sell that variety.

Use a ricer to rice the potatoes into a large bowl. If you don't have a ricer, put a quarter of the potatoes in a metal colander with holes (not a mesh colander) and push the potatoes through with a ladle or spoon. Repeat with the remaining potatoes.

Very gently, stir the butter mixture into the potatoes, and then fold in the leek mixture and pepper. Taste and adjust the seasonings, and serve right away.

Sausage and Cracker Stuffing

12 oz [340 g] crusty white bread

2 Tbsp unsalted butter

1 lb [455 g] sweet Italian sausage, casings removed

2 carrots, peeled and diced

3 celery stalks, diced

1 onion, diced

1 tsp salt

1 tsp freshly ground black pepper

2½ cups [600 ml] turkey or chicken stock, plus more as needed

8 oz [230 g] saltine crackers, crushed

½ cup [20 g] chopped chives

SERVES

15

ASSEMBLE AHEAD

1 day

PREP TIME

2 hours

At least 1 day before you're planning to bake, tear the bread into bite-size pieces. Spread the bread on a baking sheet and leave out to dry overnight, covered with a towel. (If you don't have time for this step, dry the bread in a 200°F [95°C] oven until it's crisp but not browned, stirring every 10 minutes.)

Preheat the oven to 300°F [150°C]. Butter a 9 by 13 in [23 by 33 cm] baking dish.

In a large skillet, heat the butter over medium-high heat until it melts. Add the sausage to the pan and break it apart with two forks so there aren't any huge chunks. Cook, stirring occasionally, until the sausage is browned, 6 to 8 minutes. Transfer the sausage to a very large bowl using a slotted spoon, leaving the fat in the skillet.

Adjust the heat to medium and add the carrots, celery, onion, salt, and pepper. Cook, stirring often, until the vegetables are softened but haven't colored at all, 10 to 15 minutes. Pour the stock into the pan and bring to a boil, scraping any browned bits off the bottom. Remove from the heat.

cont'd

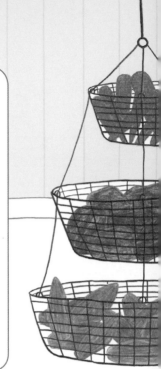

STUFFING (technically "dressing" here, but I'm of the belief that it's all "stuffing") made with saltine crackers actually goes way back. This version keeps them somewhat whole so you get more salty, flaky bites in each serving. You can easily crush them by whacking the saltines a few times in their sleeves with a rolling pin.

THE SAUSAGE makes the stuffing rich and hearty, but you could skip it and sauté the vegetables in an extra 2 Tbsp of butter to make it vegetarian.

Add the dried bread, saltines, and chives to the bowl with the sausage, and pour it over the vegetable mixture. Toss (as best you can, there's a lot of food) all the ingredients together. The bread should be pretty moist but not sopping. If it's too dry, add more stock ¼ cup [60 ml] at a time.

Transfer the stuffing to the prepared baking dish and cover with foil. Bake, undisturbed, for 40 minutes. Uncover and bake until the top is golden, 30 to 35 minutes longer. Serve warm.

Apple and Pecan Cornbread Dressing

2 cups [240 g] chopped pecans

1 recipe Black Pepper Cornbread (page 47, stuffing variation), baked 1 to 3 days in advance

2 Tbsp unsalted butter

1 onion, diced

4 celery stalks, diced

2 tsp salt

½ tsp freshly ground black pepper

2½ cups [600 ml] vegetable or chicken stock

½ cup [70 g] dried cranberries

2 apples, cored and chopped

2 eggs, lightly beaten

½ cup [20 g] chopped fresh parsley

>>

SERVES
15

MAKE THE CORNBREAD
AHEAD
3 days

ASSEMBLE AHEAD
1 day

PREP TIME
2 hours
(plus baking cornbread)

Preheat the oven to 200°F [95°C]. Butter a 9 by 13 in [23 by 33 cm] baking dish.

Spread the pecans on a baking sheet and toast in the oven, stirring occasionally, until they are slightly darkened and smell toasted, 8 to 10 minutes. Transfer to a very large bowl. Combine with the cornbread.

Raise the oven temperature to 375°F [190°C]. In a large skillet, melt the butter over medium heat. Add the onion, celery, salt, and pepper. Cook, stirring often, until the vegetables are softened but haven't colored at all, 10 to 15 minutes. Add the stock and cranberries, and bring to a boil. Carefully pour the mixture into the bowl, and add the apples, eggs, and parsley. Gently fold the mixture to combine everything and hydrate the bread.

Spread the mixture in the prepared baking dish and cover with foil. Bake, undisturbed, for 45 minutes. Remove the foil and continue baking until the stuffing is crisp on top, 20 to 25 minutes longer. Serve hot or warm.

THIS DRESSING plays up the sweetness of cornbread with the apples and dried cranberries. It's great with the Black Pepper Cornbread (page 47) cooked in the "stuffing variation." By cooking it in a sheet tray, it gets drier (here, a good thing), meaning you don't need to crisp it in the oven, and it is much easier to cut.

DESPITE WHAT I said on page 29, this is one time where you do have to use vegetable stock if you want to make it vegetarian. Try to find the best-tasting one you can.

TURKEY & MORE

Turkey Talk

THE CENTERPIECE OF THE MEAL
doesn't have to be super complicated.

||||||||||||||||||||||||||||||||||||||||||||||||||||||||||||||||||||||||||||||||||||||||||||||||||||||||||||

HERE ARE A FEW THINGS TO KEEP IN MIND:

How Much Turkey?

THE GENERAL RULE OF THUMB IS 1 LB [455 G] OF TURKEY PER PERSON. Yes, that does seem like a lot, but remember there are lots of bones and generally plenty of turkey that doesn't make it onto people's plates (bonus for you and your stock supply). Plus, people love leftovers.

Buying a turkey under or over 2 lb [910 g] of your guest list is ideal. You could buy up to 50 percent more poundage if you *really* like leftovers, but any more is overkill. If you can't find the right size turkey for your crowd, supplement the extra with braised turkey legs (page 81). You could also serve an additional "main" that's not turkey: lasagna (page 93), pork roast, pizza, whatever your stomach desires. It's your holiday!

Should You Brine?

THE SHORT ANSWER IS: YES. The long answer is: yes, but I know you don't have the fridge space to do it.

It's pretty much impossible to get the thigh and breast to finish cooking at the exact same time, and brining ensures the breast stays moist as it cooks. If you have the space and inclination, there are lots of resources online for brining. But I skip it in this book because the ability to do it safely is pretty rare.

Food Safety

FIRST, YOU MUST BUY AN INSTANT-READ THERMOMETER. You cannot tell a turkey is safely cooked any other way. The temperature you're looking for to ensure doneness without dryness is 165°F [75°C]. Always check in a few spots, and always go by the lowest temperature reading; meaning if you get reads of 170°F [77°C], 165°F [75°C], and 149°F [65°C], it's not done yet. And if that's the case, see number 3 below.

IF YOU BUY A FROZEN TURKEY, REMEMBER THESE TIMES: a turkey needs 1 day for every 4 lb [1.8 kg] to thaw in the fridge, or 30 minutes completely submerged in cold water for every 1 lb [455 g]. Plan ahead! You can't just cook your turkey longer if it's not fully thawed on Thanksgiving; you will have a turkey that's both overcooked and undercooked.

OTHER BASIC SAFETY WITH MEAT: Wash your hands often, and wash anything that the raw turkey comes into contact with. (But generally, try to make sure the raw turkey doesn't touch anything.) Once the turkey is done, it can safely sit out for up to 2 hours; after that, cover and refrigerate it.

. . . AND SOME TROUBLESHOOTING

1 ✕

IF YOUR TURKEY IS OVERCOOKED:

Double the gravy (page 86)! That will cover any dryness.

2 ✕

IF YOUR TURKEY IS UNDERCOOKED:

Cut the legs and breasts off and roast them on a baking sheet in a 375°F [190°C] oven, checking every 10 minutes, until a thermometer inserted into the thickest part of the piece registers 165°F [75°C].

3 ✕

IF THE BREAST IS FINISHED WAY AHEAD OF THE THIGH:

Try cooling it off by basting it with pan juices or stock, or cover the breast with foil until the thigh finishes cooking.

I WOULD say this is "nothing fancy," but roasting a bird big enough to feed a dozen people will always be impressive. This is your classic, no-gimmicks roast turkey—great for your first Thanksgiving or your twentieth. See How Much Turkey? on page 74 for more details about what to do if you're expecting more than fourteen people.

READ THE recipe through carefully, and double-check the math on *when* you need to buy the turkey. It needs to be fully thawed by Wednesday night if you go the frozen route. Thawing in the refrigerator is the safest option if you have the space, and a turkey this size will take at least 3 days.

Simple but Classic Roast Turkey

One 12 to 14 lb [5.4 to 6.4 kg] turkey, thawed

Salt

4 lb [1.8 kg] aromatic vegetables (carrots, onions, celery) cut into 1 in [2.5 cm] chunks (optional)

4 Tbsp [55 g] unsalted butter, at room temperature

Freshly ground black pepper

1 onion, quartered

1 head garlic, halved lengthwise

1 bunch fresh sage

2 cups [480 ml] chicken stock or dry white wine

SERVES

14

PREP TIME

5 hours

Wednesday night, make sure there is room in your fridge for the turkey setup. Place a wire rack on a baking sheet and put the turkey on top. Remove the giblets and neck from the turkey cavity and pat the turkey dry. Sprinkle the turkey with 1 Tbsp salt and rub the salt into the skin. Put the turkey, uncovered, in the fridge overnight.

Five hours before you want to serve (just to be safe), take the turkey out of the refrigerator and pat the skin dry if necessary. Let it come to room temperature, about 1 hour.

Preheat the oven to 350°F [180°C]. Transfer the turkey to a roasting pan fitted with a rack, or a pan with a layer of aromatic vegetables cut into chunks (the turkey can't be touching the bottom).

cont'd

Season the softened butter with 1 tsp salt and ½ tsp pepper, then spread it all over the turkey. Sprinkle the cavity generously with 1 tsp salt, then stuff the bird with the onion, garlic, and sage.

Transfer the bird to the oven and roast until a thermometer inserted into the meatiest part of the inner thigh—not touching the bone—registers 145°F [65°C], 1½ to 2 hours. Pour the stock into the roasting pan to prevent the juices from burning and turn the heat up to 425°F [220°C]. Cook until the skin is golden brown and a thermometer inserted into the same area registers 165°F [75°C], 15 to 25 minutes longer.

Carefully remove the vegetables from the cavity and discard. Tip the turkey so any juices run into the pan, and reserve them to make gravy (page 86). Let the turkey rest for 40 minutes, then carve and serve warm or at room temperature.

Turkey Legs Braised in White Wine

3 turkey drumsticks, about 6 lb [2.7 kg]

1 Tbsp salt

1 tsp freshly ground black pepper

3 Tbsp extra-virgin olive oil

2 large carrots, peeled and cut into chunks

1 yellow onion, cut into wedges

1 head garlic, halved horizontally

3 sprigs fresh thyme

One 750-ml bottle dry white wine

2 cups [480 ml] turkey stock, chicken stock, or water

¼ cup [10 g] chopped fresh parsley, for garnish

>>

SERVES

6 to 8

MAKE AHEAD

1 day

PREP TIME

4 hours

GF

Preheat the oven to 275°F [135°C]. Sprinkle the turkey legs on both sides with the salt and pepper.

In a large skillet, heat the oil over medium-high heat until it shimmers. Working one or two turkey legs at a time, cook, undisturbed, until the skin is a deep golden brown, 4 to 5 minutes. Turn the turkey to cook on all four "sides." Transfer the legs to a 9 by 13 in [23 by 33 cm] baking dish, fitting them in as best you can (they'll shrink as they braise). Repeat with the remaining turkey legs.

Add the carrots, onion, garlic, and thyme to the skillet and cook, stirring occasionally, until browned in spots, 8 to 10 minutes. Pour in the wine and bring to a boil, scraping any browned bits from the bottom of the skillet. Cook until the wine has reduced by about half, 5 to 7 minutes.

cont'd

Pour the mixture over the turkey legs in the baking dish. Transfer to the oven, pull out the rack, and carefully pour in the stock to come within ½ in [12 mm] of the top of the baking dish. Close the oven and cook, uncovered, until the turkey is tender and falling off the bone, 3 to 3½ hours.

Use tongs to transfer the turkey and vegetables to a serving platter, garnish with the parsley, and serve hot. You can serve the pan drippings on the side or use them to make gravy (page 86).

I'M CERTAINLY not the first person to say this, but roast turkey breast isn't as good as people think it is. Do yourself a favor and make this tender, flavorful, dark meat–only braise instead. I promise the leftovers will be even better than your standard turkey.

IF YOU have a pan that can comfortably fit more turkey legs, you can scale up the recipe. But I found that giant grocery store–size legs (as opposed to those you might find from a local farmer) were too big to fit more of them into the pan. If you can fit more, you won't need to increase any of the ingredients, except perhaps the stock.

I LOVE this "low and slow" cooking technique, but it does have one (large) caveat: it puts your oven out of commission for quite a while. Now, there are plenty of situations where this is OK—you are cooking only the turkey, you are making all stovetop sides, you have two ovens (ha, yeah right), or you already baked everything else and it just needs to be warmed before serving. If any of those apply, give this method a try. It's worth it for the very crisp skin and juicy final product.

Slow-Roasted Turkey

One 12 to 14 lb [5.4 to 6.4 kg] turkey

6 Tbsp [90 g] unsalted butter, at room temperature

1 Tbsp salt

1 tsp freshly ground black pepper

4 lb [1.8 kg] aromatic vegetables (carrots, onions, celery) cut into 1 in [2.5 cm] chunks (optional)

1 onion, quartered

6 garlic cloves

3 sprigs fresh thyme

2 sprigs fresh marjoram or oregano

4 cups [1.9 L] chicken or turkey stock

SERVES
12 to 14

PREP TIME
9 hours

GF

At least 8½ hours before you plan to eat, preheat the oven to 450°F [230°C] and bring the turkey to room temperature, about 1 hour.

In a small bowl, mix the butter, salt, and pepper. Fit a roasting pan with a rack (or spread a layer of aromatic vegetables cut into chunks across the bottom) and add the turkey, breast facing up. Rub the butter all over the turkey, and rub any extra in the cavity. Stuff the turkey with the onion, garlic, and herbs. Pour 2 cups [480 ml] water into the bottom of the pan.

Roast the turkey for 45 minutes, then turn the heat down to 250°F [120°C]. Cook, dousing the breast with a splash of stock every 45 minutes or so, until a thermometer inserted into the meatiest part of the inner thigh—not touching the bone—registers 165°F [75°C], 5½ to 6½ hours longer.

Tip the turkey so any juices run into the pan, and reserve them to make gravy (page 86). Let the turkey rest for 40 minutes, then carve and serve warm or at room temperature.

Turkey Gravy

Pan juices from roasted turkey (page 79 or 85) or Turkey Legs Braised in White Wine (page 81), strained

Turkey or chicken stock, as needed (see directions)

⅓ cup [45 g] all-purpose flour

Salt

Freshly ground black pepper

>>

SERVES

8 to 12

PREP TIME

30 minutes

If there's a lot of fat in the pan juices, skim some off the top (but not all, since there isn't any butter in this recipe). Pour the juices into a blender and add enough stock to total 4 cups [960 ml] (your blender should have markings for liquid measures). Add the flour and blend until smooth.

Transfer the mixture to a medium saucepan and bring to a boil over medium-high heat. Adjust the heat so the mixture simmers gently, and cook until it is thickened and you can no longer taste the flour, 10 to 15 minutes. Season with salt and pepper. Serve hot.

MAKING GRAVY with roux seems so daunting and time-consuming; I just go with this blender method instead. This isn't gloppy gravy, and it might seem thin when it's done, but it will thicken to a nice consistency once it's off the heat. Gravy has never been so easy.

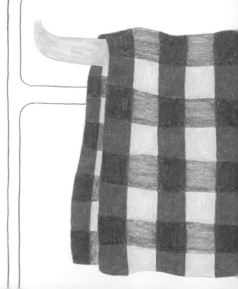

YOUR VEGETARIAN friends
deserve to have something to
pour all over their sides, too.
Show them you care with
this very flavorful gravy.

Garlic-Miso Gravy

12 oz [340 g] cremini mushrooms, trimmed and quartered

1 head garlic, halved horizontally

1 carrot, peeled and cut into chunks

1 onion, cut into chunks

2 sprigs fresh rosemary

3 Tbsp extra-virgin olive oil

1 tsp salt

¼ tsp freshly ground black pepper

½ cup [120 ml] dry white wine

2 Tbsp soy sauce

¼ cup [70 g] white or yellow miso

2 Tbsp all-purpose flour

>>>>>>>>>>>>>>>>>>>>>>>>>>>>>>>>>>>>>>>

SERVES

10

MAKE AHEAD

3 days

PREP TIME

2 hours

VEG

Preheat the oven to 400°F [200°C].

Put the vegetables and rosemary on a rimmed baking sheet and add the oil, salt, and pepper. Toss to coat. Roast, stirring once or twice, until everything is nicely browned and the garlic is caramelized, 40 to 45 minutes.

Discard the rosemary, squeeze the garlic from the skins, and add the roasted vegetables to a large pot. While the baking sheet is still hot, add the wine and scrape off any browned bits from the bottom, then add to the pot. Bring the mixture to a boil over medium-high heat and cook until the wine has almost completely evaporated, 3 to 5 minutes. Add the soy sauce and 4 cups [960 ml] water, and bring to a boil. Adjust the heat and simmer for 10 minutes to let the flavors mingle.

Turn off the heat, and add the miso and flour. Carefully purée everything in the pot using an immersion blender (or let the mixture cool, transfer to a blender, and work *very* carefully in batches). Strain the mixture through a fine-mesh sieve (fussy but a necessary step!). At this point you can cool the gravy and store for up to 3 days.

Return the gravy to the pot and bring to a boil over high heat. Adjust the heat to medium, and simmer until the gravy thickens and you can no longer taste the flour, 10 to 15 minutes. Serve hot.

Butternut Squash, Blue Cheese, and Radicchio Tart

---

1 small butternut squash, peeled, halved, and seeded

1 recipe Pie Dough (page 102), chilled for at least 1 hour and unrolled

½ cup [120 ml] heavy cream

1 tsp salt, plus more for seasoning

½ tsp freshly ground black pepper, plus more for seasoning

8 oz [230 g] creamy blue cheese, crumbled

1 egg, beaten

1 radicchio head, leaves separated

1 Tbsp extra-virgin olive oil

>>

SERVES
12

MAKE SQUASH AHEAD
3 days

MAKE DOUGH AHEAD
3 days

PREP TIME
2 hours
(plus making pie dough)

VEG

Preheat the oven to 350°F [180°C].

Using a mandoline or very sharp knife, slice the butternut squash as thinly as you can manage. Put the squash in a large bowl. (You can do this up to 3 days ahead of time; just keep the squash tightly covered.)

Lightly flour your work surface and put the dough on top. Starting from the center of the dough, push the rolling pin away from you in firm strokes, rotating the dough 45 degrees every two strokes, until the dough forms an oval about ¼ in [6 mm] thick and roughly 13 by 17 in [33 by 43 cm]. Carefully transfer the dough to a piece of parchment, then transfer the parchment to a baking sheet.

cont'd

I'D MAKE this for any fall or winter special occasion. It's a lovely vegetarian main, though no one would object to you serving this *and* turkey.

Brush the dough with enough cream to lightly coat the surface, and then pour the remainder of the cream into the bowl with the squash. Season the squash with the salt and pepper, and then add the blue cheese. Gently toss everything to coat.

Leaving a 2 in [5 cm] border all around, put the squash mixture onto the dough, trying to keep the filling an even thickness. Fold the excess dough up and over the filling. Brush the tart with the beaten egg. Bake for 45 minutes.

Meanwhile, mix the radicchio with the olive oil and a pinch of salt and pepper. Carefully top the tart with the radicchio after the first 45 minutes, taking care not to cover the crust and leaving any liquid in the bowl. Continue baking until the squash is tender, the radicchio is wilted, and the crust is a deep golden color, 20 to 25 minutes longer.

Transfer the pan to a cooling rack and let set for at least 15 minutes before slicing and serving warm or at room temperature.

Sage and Mushroom Lasagna

MUSHROOM FILLING

3 Tbsp unsalted butter

2 lb [910 g] flavorful mixed mushrooms (such as cremini, shiitake, or any fancy specialty ones you might find), roughly chopped

1 tsp salt

½ tsp freshly ground black pepper

SAGE BÉCHAMEL

4 cups [960 ml] whole milk

2 sprigs fresh sage

½ cup [110 g] unsalted butter

1 shallot, minced

½ cup [70 g] all-purpose flour

1 tsp salt

½ tsp freshly ground black pepper

1½ lb [680 g] fresh pasta sheets, or one 9 oz [255 g] box no-boil lasagna noodles

4½ cups [360 g] grated Gruyère cheese

12 fresh sage leaves

>>>

SERVES

12

MAKE FILLING AHEAD

3 days

MAKE BÉCHAMEL AHEAD

3 days

ASSEMBLE AHEAD

1 day

PREP TIME

2 hours

VEG

TO MAKE THE MUSHROOM FILLING: In a large sauté pan, melt the butter over medium-high heat, then add the mushrooms, season with the salt and pepper, and stir. Cover the pan and cook until the mushrooms have released most of their liquid, 5 to 8 minutes. Uncover the pan and cook, stirring only occasionally, until the liquid has cooked off and the pan is dry, up to 20 minutes depending on the mushrooms. At this point, start stirring even less to let the mushrooms crisp. When every mushroom is golden on at least one side, remove from the heat. You can cool and refrigerate the mushroom mixture for up to 3 days.

cont'd

TO MAKE THE BÉCHAMEL: In a small saucepan, heat the milk and sage until just steaming. Do not let it boil. In a medium saucepan, melt the butter over medium heat, add the shallot, and cook until translucent, 3 to 5 minutes. Add the flour and cook, whisking constantly, until the flour and butter are incorporated and the flour is cooked, 4 to 5 minutes. (You'll know the flour is ready if you—carefully—taste a little and it no longer tastes raw.) Add the warm milk ½ cup [120 ml] at a time, whisking constantly so the milk is incorporated before adding any more, and continue until you've used all the milk; discard the sage sprigs. Cook the mixture until it has thickened and has a saucy consistency, 2 to 3 minutes. Add the salt and pepper, taste, and add more if necessary. Keep warm, or cool and refrigerate for up to 3 days.

Preheat the oven to 375°F [190°C]. Butter a 9 by 13 in [23 by 33 cm] baking dish.

Spread ¼ cup [60 ml] of the béchamel on the bottom of the pan, then cover with lasagna sheets, making sure they don't overlap. Spread 1 cup [240 ml] béchamel on the noodles, then top with a quarter of the cooked mushrooms and 1 cup [80 g] of the Gruyère. Repeat three more times and top with a final layer of noodles. Sprinkle the remaining ½ cup [40 g] Gruyère on the noodles and pour over the remaining béchamel. Arrange the sage leaves on top of the lasagna. (The lasagna can be covered tightly and refrigerated at this point for up to 1 day. Let it come to room temperature for about an hour before proceeding.)

Bake, covered with foil, for 30 minutes. Uncover and cook until the top is browned and the sauce is bubbling, 20 to 30 minutes longer. Let it set for 10 minutes before slicing and serving hot.

NOWHERE CLOSE to traditional, lasagna is a wonderful option for Thanksgiving. This version is vegetarian and full of rich fall flavors, like sage-infused béchamel, crisp pan-roasted mushrooms, and plenty of Gruyère cheese. As a bonus, you can cook the components throughout the week when you have time, assemble the lasagna up to a day before your Friendsgiving dinner, and then only have it in the oven for about an hour. It's (almost) easy when you spread out the preparation like that.

LASAGNA IS a special-occasion food, so I like to use fresh pasta sheets. If you can't find them at your grocery store, go for no-boil noodles. Not my favorite, but boiling noodles is such a pain that I'll do everything I can to avoid it.

All This Food Ready

It takes a little coordination, but nothing too crazy.

Thankfully, you don't need to have restaurant training to ensure all the food hits the table at the same time.

Prep Ahead

OK, this is something I *did* learn working in restaurants, but it translates very well at home. In the days and nights leading up to Thanksgiving, chop everything you can. Put the measured ingredients into storage containers with the name of the dish they're for, and everything will be ready to dump and cook on Thursday.

Cook What You Can in Advance

Some dishes store better than others. Read the recipes once through, and then plan what you can make a few days ahead (cranberries, appetizers) and what you can't (mashed potatoes, turkey). But don't go crazy. I have a friend who said her grandmother used to cook everything two weeks in advance and freeze it all. The whole family dreaded going to her house for Thanksgiving.

Make an Oven Schedule

A little type A? Yes. But having an idea of what goes into the oven and when on Thanksgiving is going to save you from potential heartbreak or mutiny when dinnertime comes and goes. Figure out when the turkey needs to be in the oven and organize around that. Plan on having the oven at 250°F [120°C] when guests start arriving so you can warm dishes if need be.

It Doesn't All Have to Be *Hot*-Hot

Look, no one's going to begrudge you providing a Thanksgiving dinner with some dishes that are just warm. As long as everything is close to the temperature it's supposed to be (and everything that needs to be cooked is no longer raw), you'll be fine. And if your friends complain, that's rude (and they don't need to come back next year).

X

PIES PIES PIES

Pie Dough

>>

2½ cups [350 g] all-purpose flour

1 Tbsp sugar

1 tsp salt

1 cup [220 g] unsalted butter, very cold and cubed

¼ cup [60 ml] vodka, very cold

In a large bowl, mix the flour, sugar, and salt with a fork. Add the butter and use two forks or a pastry cutter to work the butter into the flour until most of the butter is broken up into very small pieces (only a few pea-size pieces) and the mixture looks crumbly.

In a measuring cup with a spout, mix the vodka with ¼ cup [60 ml] cold water and a large handful of ice. Pour a little of the wet mixture onto the dry mixture and incorporate with the pastry cutter or a fork. Continue adding small amounts of liquid and incorporating it until you can pinch a little of the mixture between your fingers and it holds together (you might not use all the liquid). The dough won't be in one ball yet, but there shouldn't be any pockets of dry flour, nor should it be sticky. Press the dough together, and then wrap it tightly with plastic wrap. Chill for at least 1 hour and up to 3 days (you'll be surprised how the flour continues to hydrate while it rests).

NOTE: If you're making just the Sweet Potato Pie with Marshmallow Fluff (page 113), you can freeze half of the dough—tightly wrapped—for up to 1 month.

Troubleshooting

Don't be alarmed by the pie dough if you're used to adding much more water! I like to make my dough on the *very* dry side. It's flakier that way, if a little harder to work with. If you find the mixture is still a little crumbly after resting, it usually will come together as it warms up and you start working with it. You can always smoosh any crumbly bits back into the main dough round.

PREVENT SAD PIE

USE COLD INGREDIENTS
There are a million articles about why, and they're all correct.

DON'T OVERWORK THE DOUGH
It will only turn out tough. As soon as you can pinch the dough and it holds together (and there are no pockets of dry flour), it's done. Step away.

USE AS LITTLE LIQUID AS POSSIBLE
More will also make the dough tough.

USE A GLASS BAKING DISH
So you can see the bottom and know it's fully cooked.

YOU REALLY CAN'T OVERCOOK PIE DOUGH
So if you're not sure about your fruit pie (custard is a whole different ball game), go ahead and bake it for 10 minutes longer.

IF YOU DON'T HAVE VODKA
You can substitute apple cider vinegar, but both are better options than plain water.

THIS IS my absolute favorite kind of pie. And the end of Concord grape season just so happens to be mid-November in the Northeast, so you should be able to find them easily throughout the rest of the country. If you're nervous, talk to the grower at the farmers' market or supermarket buyer, and maybe they can set some aside for you the week before Thanksgiving. Any favors that can be pulled are definitely worth it.

THE ADDITION of allspice comes from the version at the wonderful pie shop Four & Twenty Blackbirds in Brooklyn, New York.

Concord Grape Pie

2 lb [910 g] Concord grapes

1 cup [200 g] lightly packed
light brown sugar

3 Tbsp cornstarch

½ tsp salt

½ tsp allspice

1 recipe Pie Dough
(page 102)

1 egg, lightly beaten

1 Tbsp granulated sugar

>>

SERVES
8 to 10

MAKE FILLING AHEAD
2 days

BAKE AHEAD
1 day

PREP TIME
2½ hours
(plus making pie dough)

TIME TO COOL
4 hours

VEG

This is the fun part (jk): remove each grape from the stem and squeeze the grape so the flesh comes away from the skin. Put the fruit in one bowl and the skins in another. Now repeat that with entire 2 lb [910 g] of grapes.

In a large saucepan over medium heat, cook the fruit until it's mostly broken down, 8 to 10 minutes. Pour the mixture through a sieve into a clean bowl, and press on the seeds until you get as much of the juice and pulp through as possible. Discard the seeds. Roughly chop the skins (I use kitchen shears and cut them in the bowl to keep my cutting board from turning purple). Add them to the cooked fruit and mix well.

In a small bowl, whisk together the brown sugar, cornstarch, salt, and allspice. Add the mixture to the grapes and stir until no lumps remain. At this point you can refrigerate the mixture for up to 2 days. Let it cool while you roll the dough.

cont'd

Lightly flour your work surface. Cut the dough in half and form both halves into rounds; wrap the half you're not working with, and keep it in the fridge. Starting from the center of the dough, push the rolling pin away from you in firm strokes, rotating the dough 45 degrees every two strokes (and adding flour as necessary to prevent the dough from sticking), until the dough forms an even circle that is about 13 in [33 cm] in diameter. Carefully transfer the dough to a 9 in [23 cm] pie pan and gently press into place. Roll out the remaining dough to the same size.

Pour the grape mixture into the prepared pie pan, carefully drape the other dough round over the pie, and crimp the edges in whatever style you prefer, then trim the excess dough. Brush the dough with the beaten egg, and then sprinkle with the granulated sugar. Using a sharp, thin-bladed knife, carefully cut four or five vents in the top dough. Chill for 30 minutes before baking.

Preheat the oven to 400°F [200°C].

Put the pie pan on a baking sheet and bake until the pastry is beginning to color, 20 to 25 minutes. Turn the oven down to 350°F [180°C] and continue baking until the crust is well browned and the juices are bubbling and syrupy, 50 to 60 minutes longer.

Cool completely on a wire rack (at least 4 hours) before cutting and serving. The pie can be covered with foil and stored at room temperature for up to 2 days.

Spiced Caramel Apple Pie

SPICED CARAMEL

1 cup [200 g] granulated sugar

½ cup [110 g] unsalted butter, cubed

½ cup [120 ml] heavy cream

1 tsp ground cardamom

½ tsp salt

PIE

Juice of 2 lemons

2½ lb [1.2 kg] Granny Smith apples

½ tsp salt

1 recipe Pie Dough (page 102)

¼ cup [50 g] lightly packed light brown sugar

1 Tbsp cornstarch

1 tsp ground cinnamon

1 egg, lightly beaten

1 Tbsp granulated sugar

> >

SERVES
8 to 10

MAKE CARAMEL AHEAD
3 days

BAKE AHEAD
1 day

PREP TIME
3 hours
(plus making pie dough)

TIME TO COOL
4 hours

TO MAKE THE CARAMEL: In a heavy-bottomed medium saucepan, combine the granulated sugar and ¼ cup [60 ml] water, and stir so the sugar is completely hydrated. Cook over medium-low heat until the sugar dissolves, add the butter, and bring the mixture to a simmer. Cook, swirling the pan but not stirring, until the mixture is the color of maple syrup (depending on your pan this could take anywhere from 20 to 35 minutes; go by the color to know when it's ready). Remove from the heat and carefully pour in the cream. Add the cardamom and salt, and whisk to combine. Let cool completely.

cont'd

TO MAKE THE PIE: Put the lemon juice in a large bowl. Working with one apple at a time, peel it, cut around the core, and thinly slice, adding the slices to the bowl as you go and tossing with the lemon juice so they don't brown. When you are finished, add the salt and toss to mix with the apples. Let the mixture macerate, stirring occasionally, for about 20 minutes.

Lightly flour your work surface. Cut the dough in half and form both halves into rounds; wrap the half you're not working with, and keep it in the fridge. Starting from the center of the dough, push the rolling pin away from you in firm strokes, rotating the dough 45 degrees every two strokes (and adding flour as necessary to prevent the dough from sticking), until the dough forms an even circle that is about 13 in [33 cm] in diameter. Carefully transfer the dough to a 9 in [23 cm] pie pan and gently press into place. Roll out the remaining dough to the same size.

Combine the brown sugar, cornstarch, and cinnamon in a small bowl. Pour off any excess juices from the apples, add the sugar mixture, and toss to coat. Pile the apple mixture high into the prepared pie pan and pour 2/3 cup [160 ml] of the spiced caramel over the apples. Carefully drape the other dough round over the pie and fold the excess dough up and in to make the edge. Crimp in whatever style you prefer. Brush the dough with the beaten egg, and then sprinkle with the granulated sugar. Using a sharp, thin-bladed knife, carefully cut four or five vents in the top dough. Chill for 30 minutes before baking.

Preheat the oven to 400°F [200°C].

Put the pie pan on a baking sheet and bake until the pastry is beginning to color, 20 to 25 minutes. Turn the oven down to 350°F [180°C] and continue baking until the crust is well browned and the juices are bubbling and syrupy, 50 to 60 minutes longer.

Cool completely on a wire rack (at least 4 hours) before cutting and serving. The pie can be covered and stored at room temperature for up to 2 days.

I FIGURE you need one pie option that doesn't stray too far from tradition. You can't go wrong with apple, here made just a little sweeter with caramel and more interesting with cardamom.

I DIDN'T grow up in a sweet-potato-casserole- or sweet-potato-pie-family, but that doesn't stop me from loving the idea of both. This pie takes the sweet potato pie—similar to, if not better than, pumpkin pie—and adds homemade marshmallow fluff that turns an irresistible golden color when you broil it. The recipe makes a lot more marshmallow fluff than you need. Unfortunately, it can't be scaled, but you could probably find a guest or two who'd be happy to take some home. Or just make two of the same pie.

THE CARAMELIZED filling technique comes from the classic and very delicious pumpkin pie recipe by Meta Given.

Sweet Potato Pie with Marshmallow Fluff

½ recipe Pie Dough (page 102)

FILLING

3 medium sweet potatoes, peeled and cut into chunks

2 Tbsp unsalted butter, melted

1 tsp salt

½ cup [100 g] lightly packed light brown sugar

1 tsp ground cinnamon

½ tsp ground ginger

¼ tsp ground nutmeg

1½ cups [360 ml] half-and-half

3 egg yolks (save the whites for the marshmallow fluff)

MARSHMALLOW FLUFF

3 egg whites

½ tsp cream of tartar

⅔ cup [160 ml] light corn syrup

¼ cup [50 g] granulated sugar

1 tsp vanilla extract

>>>

SERVES
8 to 10

MAKE FILLING AHEAD
2 days

MAKE FLUFF AHEAD
8 hours

BAKE AHEAD
1 day

PREP TIME
3 hours
(plus making pie dough)

TIME TO COOL
4 hours

Lightly flour your work surface. Starting from the center of the dough, push the rolling pin away from you in firm strokes, rotating the dough 45 degrees every two strokes (and adding flour as necessary to prevent the dough from sticking), until the dough forms an even circle about 13 in [33 cm] in diameter. Carefully transfer the dough to a 9 in [23 cm] pie pan and fold the excess dough over and in to make the edge. Crimp in whatever style you like. Chill for at least 30 minutes before baking.

Preheat the oven to 350°F [180°C] and position the rack in the middle.

cont'd

Line the crust with aluminum foil and fill at least halfway up (preferably more) with pie weights or dried beans. Bake for 25 minutes. Remove the foil and weights, and let the crust cool while you make the filling.

TO MAKE THE FILLING: In a large bowl, toss the potatoes with the butter and ½ tsp of the salt. Spread the potatoes in one layer on a rimmed baking sheet. Roast, stirring every 10 to 15 minutes, until the potatoes are soft and a little browned, but haven't taken on much color, 45 to 55 minutes. Transfer to a food processor and purée, or mash with a wooden spoon. Raise the oven temperature to 400°F [200°C].

In a heavy-bottomed skillet over medium-high heat, cook the puréed potatoes, stirring constantly, until the mixture is dry and caramelized, 8 to 10 minutes. Stir in the remaining ½ tsp salt, the brown sugar, spices, half-and-half, and egg yolks. Pour the mixture into the prepared pie crust and immediately transfer to the oven.

Bake until the filling is set around the edges and the center is only a little wobbly, 35 to 40 minutes. Transfer the pie to a rack and let cool completely, about 4 hours. (At this point you can wrap the pie tightly and store at room temperature for up to 1 day.)

MEANWHILE, MAKE THE MARSHMALLOW FLUFF: In a stand mixer fitted with the whisk attachment, or a large bowl with a hand mixer, beat the egg whites and cream of tartar on medium-high speed until they reach soft-peak stage, 2 to 3 minutes. Turn off the machine but keep the setup ready.

In a small saucepan with a candy thermometer attached, combine the corn syrup and granulated sugar, and stir until completely combined. Cook the mixture over medium-high heat, stirring constantly, until it reaches 238°F [114°C]. Immediately turn the stand mixer to medium-low, and begin pouring the hot sugar mixture in a steady stream so it hits the egg whites and not the bowl (this is very important). Raise the speed to medium-high, add the vanilla, and whisk the mixture until it's glossy and has cooled slightly, 1 to 2 minutes. Use right away, or transfer to an airtight container and refrigerate for up to 8 hours.

Right before you're ready to serve, heat the broiler and set the rack as far away as you can if it's a drawer-style broiler, and about 8 in [20 cm] if it's at the top of your oven. Spread a 1 in [2.5 cm] layer of fluff over the filling but not the crust. Put the pie under the broiler and toast—watching constantly and turning the pie so it colors evenly—until the marshmallow is browned in spots. Slice the pie and serve.

MENU SUGGESTIONS

MENU FOR 4

Sage Fried Almonds   25

Panfried Green Beans with Mushrooms   56

Crème Fraîche and Leek Mashed Potatoes   64

Turkey Legs Braised in White Wine   81

Sweet Potato Pie with Marshmallow Fluff   113

MENU FOR 8

Olives and crudités

Chicory and Apple Salad with Sherry Vinaigrette   38

Sautéed Brussels Sprouts with Pine Nuts   53

Sweet Potatoes au Gratin   63

Crème Fraîche and Leek Mashed Potatoes   64

Sausage and Cracker Stuffing   67

Simple but Classic Roast Turkey   79

Turkey Gravy   86

Spiced Caramel Apple Pie   109

Vanilla ice cream

MENU FOR 12

Rosemary Old-Fashioneds for a Crowd   21

Fig and Olive Relish   22

Pull-Apart Rolls   27

Cranberry Sauce with Candied Ginger   41

Roasted Pumpkin with Bacon and Dates   54

Panfried Green Beans with Mushrooms   56

Crème Fraîche and Leek Mashed Potatoes   64

Apple and Pecan Cornbread Dressing   70

Slow-Roasted Turkey   85

Turkey Gravy   86

Spiced Caramel Apple Pie   109

Sweet Potato Pie with Marshmallow Fluff   113

MOST IMPRESSIVE POTLUCK GUEST

Concord Grape Pie   107

Wine

VEGETARIAN MENU

Sage Fried Almonds   25

Chicory and Apple Salad with Sherry Vinaigrette   38

Creamed Kale and Collards   49

Panfried Green Beans with Mushrooms   56

Crème Fraîche and Leek Mashed Potatoes   64

Garlic-Miso Gravy   89

Butternut Squash, Blue Cheese, and Radicchio Tart   90

Concord Grape Pie   107

QUICK (RELATIVELY) MENU

Olives and mixed nuts

Black Pepper Cornbread   47

Sautéed Brussels Sprouts with Pine Nuts   53

Panfried Green Beans with Mushrooms   56

Turkey Legs Braised in White Wine   81

Store-bought pie

Whipped cream

BUCKING TRADITION

Rosemary Old-Fashioneds for a Crowd   21

Fig and Olive Relish   22

Chicory and Apple Salad with Sherry Vinaigrette   38

Sautéed Brussels Sprouts with Pine Nuts   53

Turkey Legs Braised in White Wine   81

Sage and Mushroom Lasagna   93

Concord Grape Pie   107

PARTIAL POTLUCK

Apple and Pecan Cornbread Dressing   70

Slow-Roasted Turkey   85

Turkey Gravy   86

Butternut Squash, Blue Cheese,
and Radicchio Tart   90

Guests provide the rest

SAVE ROOM FOR THE GOOD STUFF

Sage Fried Almonds   25

Creamed Kale and Collards   49

Roasted Pumpkin with Bacon and Dates   54

Simple but Classic Roast Turkey   79

Turkey Gravy   86

Concord Grape Pie   107

Spiced Caramel Apple Pie   109

Sweet Potato Pie with Marshmallow Fluff   113

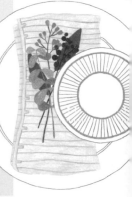

JUST THE BASICS

Cranberry Sauce with Candied Ginger   41

Panfried Green Beans with Mushrooms   56

Crème Fraîche and Leek Mashed Potatoes   64

Sausage and Cracker Stuffing   67

Simple but Classic Roast Turkey   79

Turkey Gravy   86

Sweet Potato Pie with Marshmallow Fluff   113

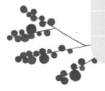

INDEX

ACKNOWLEDGMENTS

Thanks to anyone who has made a hand turkey at a Friendsgiving past. (I've kept them all.) To James and Pat for being at Friendsgivings from the beginning, and in the decade plus (!) since.

Kat, Dan, and Waffles for letting me test recipes in your kitchen when my refrigerator died, then letting me leave ten servings of turkey there.

Amir for your air-conditioned kitchen, plenty of tasting notes, and lots of seltzer water along the way.

Karina, Pete, Caitlin, Haale, and Dave for being troopers and eating a full Thanksgiving meal in 90 degree heat. Then taking home all the stuffing.

The Meat Hook for being the only place to buy turkey in August and having one ready for me every Friday throughout the month.

Caroline Schiff and Grace Rosanova for testing recipes when I needed to just not be the one to do it anymore.

Kristen Miglore, Mark Bittman, Kerri Conan, and JJ Goode for being generous with their knowledge and guidance, and helping me turn this crazy cookbook-writing idea into reality.

Angela Miller for support through every step of the process.

Melanie Gandyra for the beautiful illustrations that make the book come alive (and that I want to frame and put up all over my apartment).

Deanne Katz for reaching out to me with this perfect opportunity. I think it all worked out quite nicely!

And to Annie, Mom, and Dad for the first eighteen wonderful Thanksgivings (and all the other days of the year, too).